Melodious and Progressi
For Flute

IN C MAJOR

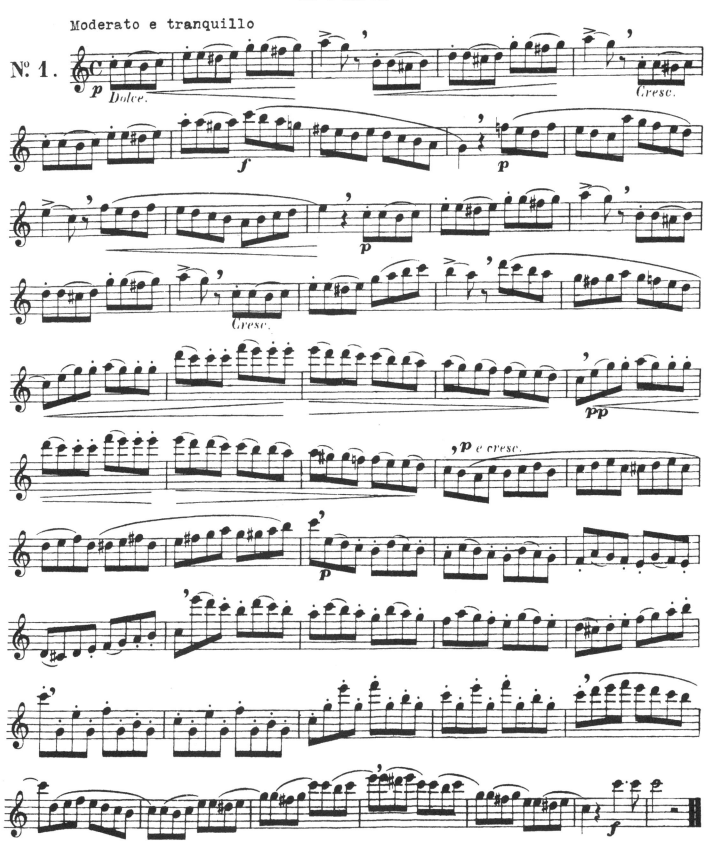

B 413

EN FA MAJEUR.

Andantino.

N.º 2.

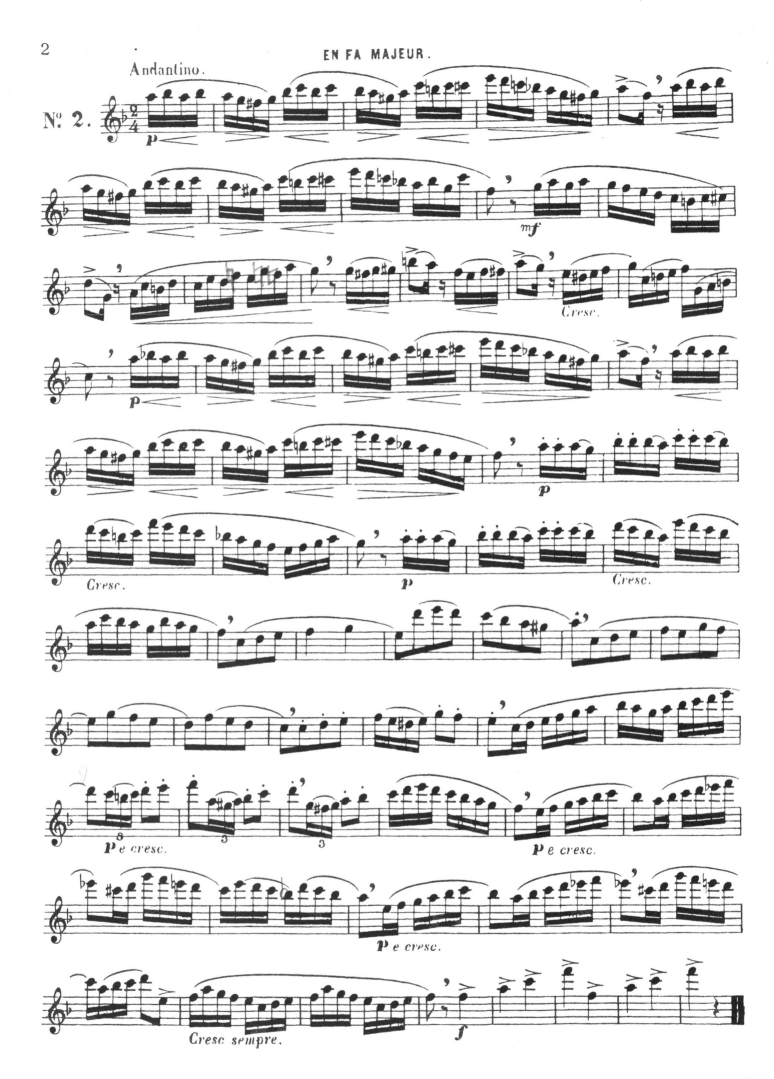

Allegretto.

N.º 3.

Con grazia.

P e cresc.

4

Tempo di Valzer.

EN FA # MINEUR.

№ 4

EN LA MAJEUR.

N.º 6

Largo cantabile.

Dolce.

Dim.

Dim. sempre e rallent.

Allegro moderato.

EN SI MINEUR.

N.º **8**.

N.º 9

Molto vivace.

EN MI MAJEUR.

Scherzando.

EN SOL MINEUR

Allegretto.

10

Tempo di Gavotte

Vivo

Tempo I

dolce

Lento—Melody by Massenet

in 4

molto rit. *a tempo*

molto espressivo

allarg. *perdendosi*

ETUDE in C MAJOR

Moderato (In 1)

A. Terschak. Op. 131 B.

This is an excellent study for double tonguing.

14

ETUDE in A MINOR

Moderato.

ETUDE in G MAJOR

Moderato.

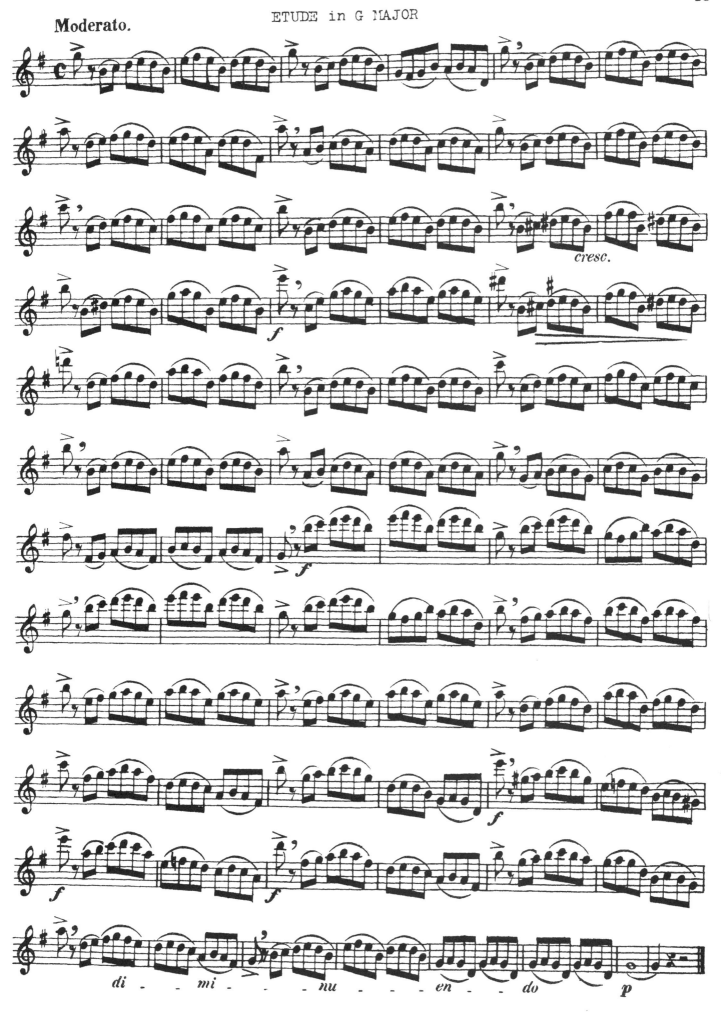

cresc.

di — — mi — — nu — — en — — do   p

Moderato.

ETUDE in D MAJOR

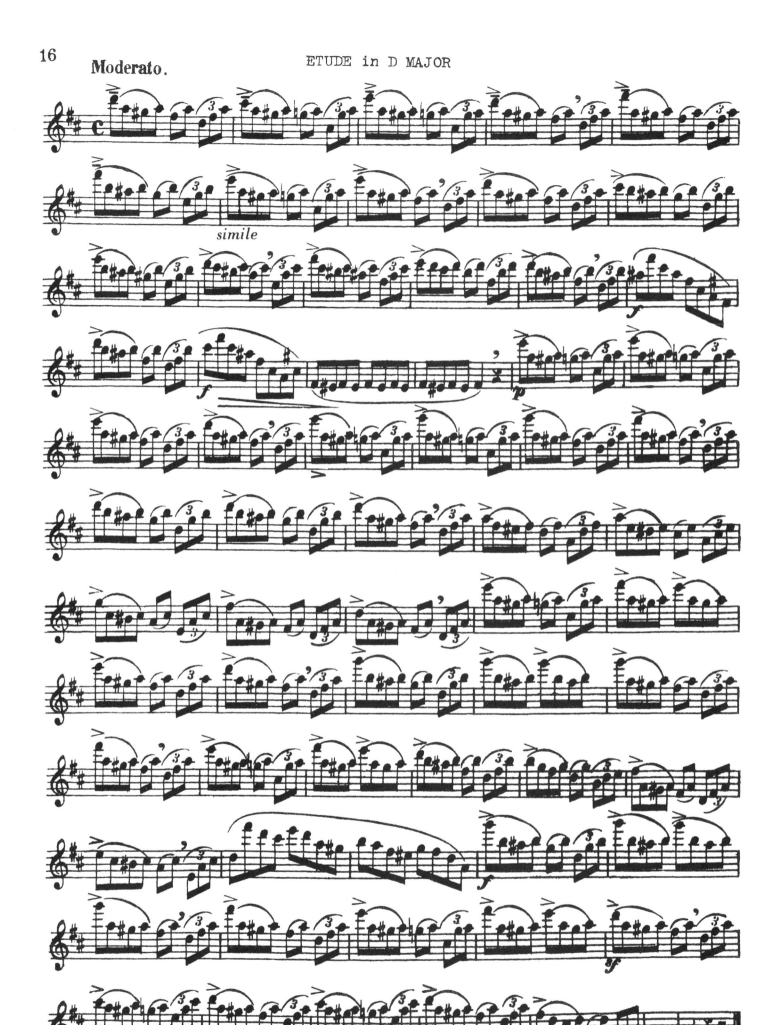

ETUDE in A MAJOR

Moderato.

ETUDE in B Flat MAJOR

15 Petites Etudes Mélodiques
by E. KÖHLER, Op 33, Book I

Allegretto.

2.

6.

Allegro moderato.

8.

Allegro.

11.

ben legato.

18 Studies For Flute
by JOACHIM ANDERSEN, Op.41

No. 3. Andantino.

№4. Allegro animato. (In 2)

№ 5. Allegretto.

Nº 6. Andantino. (In 6)

No. 7 Moderato

This is an excellent study for triple-tonguing.

Nº 8. Allegretto. (In One)

No 9. Allegro.

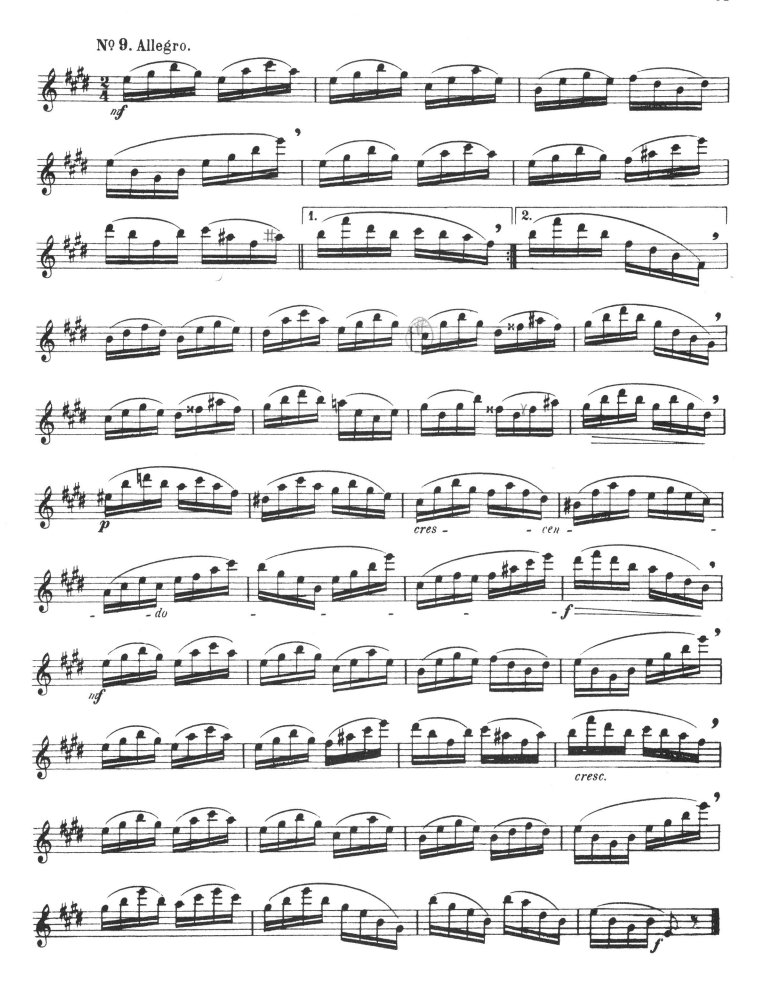

Nº 10. Adagio. (In 9)

№ 11. Moderato.

Nº 12. Andantino. (In 3)

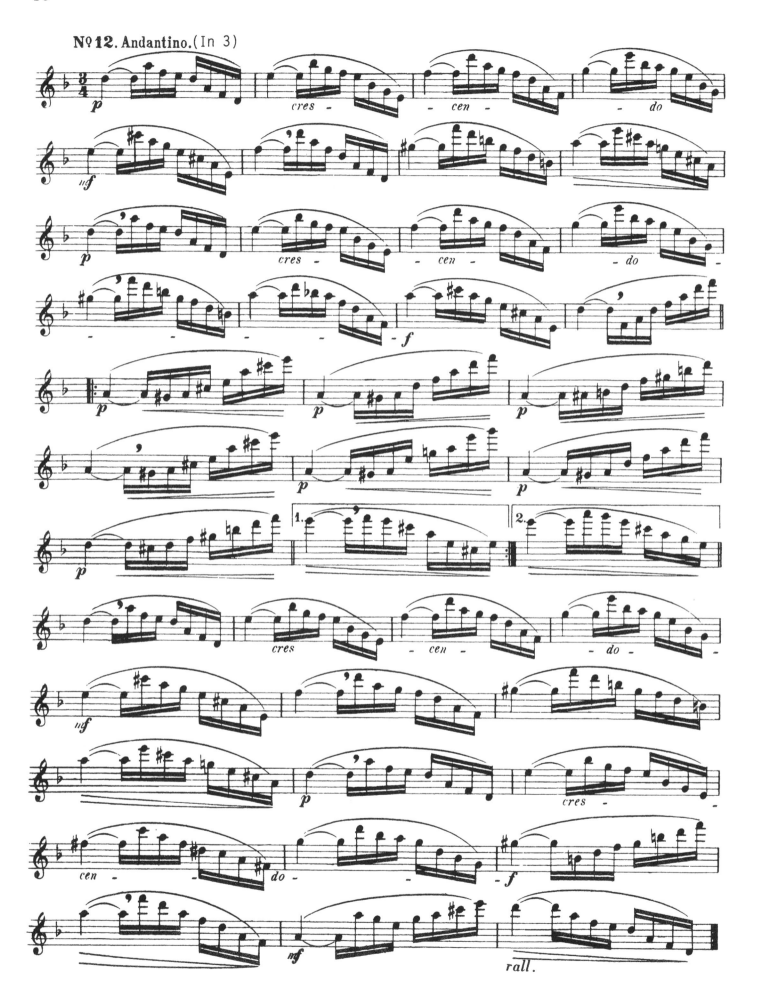

№ 13. Allegretto.

Nº 14. Andante *molto* (in 3)

Nº **15**. Lento. (In 9)

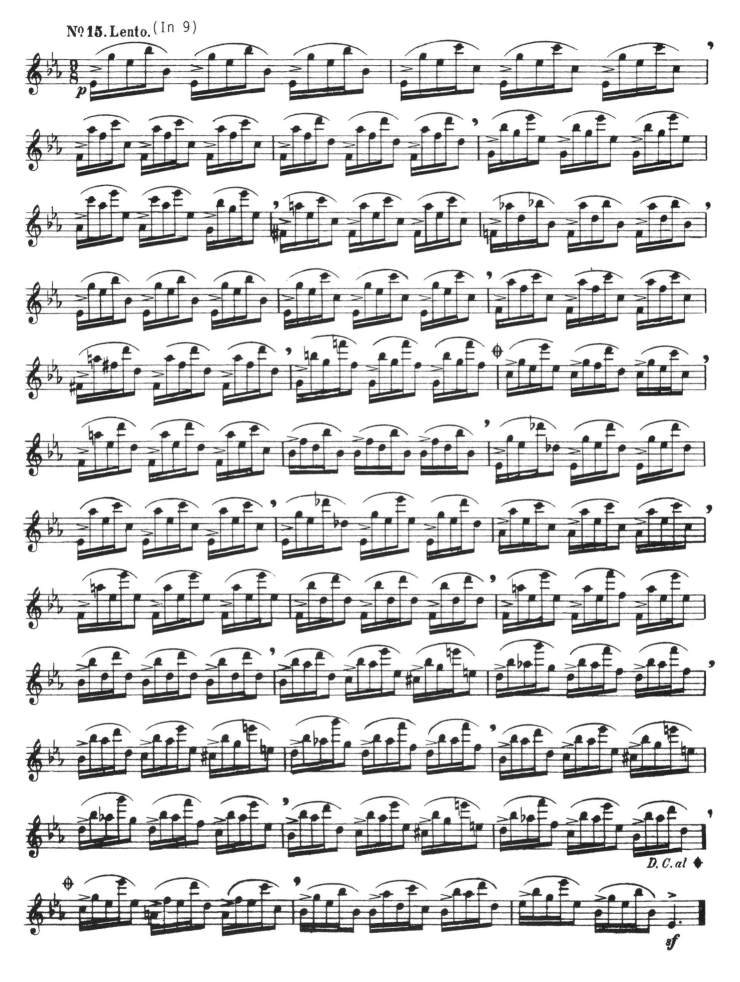

Nº 18. Allegro. (In 4)

(triple-tonguing)

50

24 Progressive Studies for the Flute

By JOACHIM ANDERSEN, Op.33

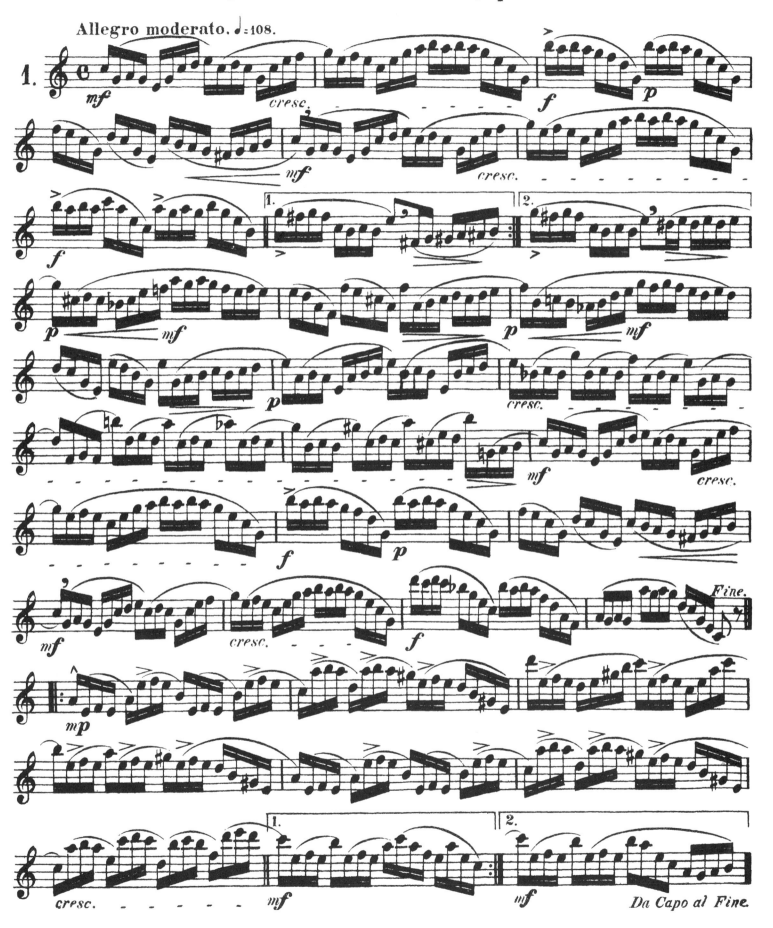

Exercises on Trills.

EXERCISES on TONGUING (DOUBLE STACCATO)

The double tonguing is of great assistance in the execution of scales or arpeggios, in the binaire rhythm. In order to execute this exercise with precision, it must be practised slowly; the student should first strive to pronounce with perfect equality the syllables tu ku tu ku tu ku etc...

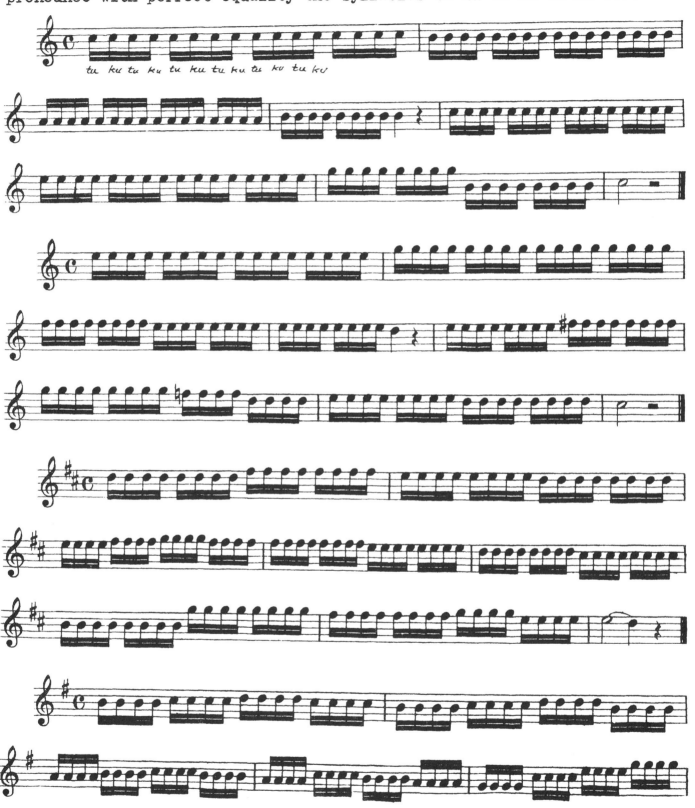

Major and Minor (Harmonic) Scales

1ʳᵉ SERIES

2ᵉ SERIES

MELODIC MINOR and ANTIQUE SCALES

(MINEUR MELODIQUE)

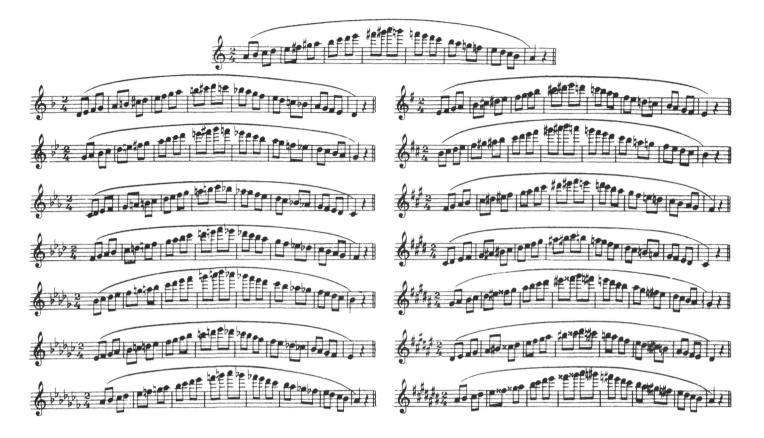

(MINEUR ANTIQUE)